DATE DUE			

599.2
WOO

15537
Woodward, John.

Kangaroos

MESA VERDE MIDDLE SCHOOL
POWAY UNIFIED SCHOOL DISTRICT

ENDANGERED!

KANGAROOS

John Woodward

Series Consultant: James G. Doherty
General Curator, The Bronx Zoo, New York

BENCHMARK BOOKS

MARSHALL CAVENDISH

NEW YORK

Benchmark Books
Marshall Cavendish Corporation
99 White Plains Road
Tarrytown, New York 10591-9001

Library of Congress Cataloging-in-Publication Data

Woodward, John, 1954-
    Kangaroos / by John Woodward.
        p.   cm. — (Endangered!)
    Includes index.
    Summary: Describes the physical characteristics, habitat, and
behavior of kangaroos living, often against all odds, in Australia
and New Guinea.
    ISBN 0-7614-0295-0
    1. Kangaroos—Juvenile literature. 2. Endangered species—
Juvenile literature. [1. Kangaroos. 2. Endangered species.]
I. Title. II. Series.
QL737.M35W66 1997
599.2—dc20   96-7222
                                                       CIP
                                                        AC

Printed and bound in the United States

PICTURE CREDITS
The publishers would like to thank the Frank Lane Picture Agency (FLPA) for
supplying all the photographs used in this book except for the following: 7, 20,
22, 23, 24 Ardea; 10, 14, 19 Bruce Coleman Ltd; 18, 21 Oxford Scientific
Films; 5 Silvestris (via FLPA); 27 Sunset (via FLPA).

Series created by Brown Packaging

Front cover: Red kangaroo.
Title page: Gray kangaroo.
Back cover: Red kangaroo with joey in pouch.

Contents

Introduction

When you hear the word "kangaroo," you probably think of a large animal, as tall as a person, bounding across the Australian plains or hopping around with a little baby called a joey peering from its pouch. There are big, fast kangaroos like this, but there are many others – about 60 different **species**. Some are hardly bigger than rats and are known as rat kangaroos. Amazingly, some climb trees, so these are known as tree kangaroos. Many are called wallabies, and others have strange names – like the quokka, warabi, and nabarlek.

A family of red kangaroos watches the camera. Reds are the largest kangaroos.

4

Kangaroos are extraordinary animals. Instead of walking or running, they hop. Believe it or not, hopping uses less energy than running, so a big kangaroo can move very fast without getting tired. A red kangaroo can leap over 30 feet (9 m) in one bound and can reach speeds of 35 miles per hour (56 km/h).

When it wants to move slowly, a kangaroo uses its strong tail as an extra "leg." The kangaroo puts its weight on its tail and slim front legs, lifts both back legs off the

The quokka is a small kangaroo about 33 inches (84 cm) long from tip of nose to tip of tail. It lives in southwest Australia.

ground and swings them forward before putting them down again. This looks awkward, but it doesn't seem to bother the kangaroo.

Most kangaroos live in Australia, but some live on the nearby island of New Guinea. Since Australia has been surrounded by water for millions of years, its animals have **evolved** in different ways from elsewhere in the world. One of the most important differences is that most Australian **mammals**, including kangaroos, raise their young in a special way. Instead of staying in its mother's body until it is quite big – like a baby bear or human, for example – a baby kangaroo is born very, very tiny. With its eyes still closed, it climbs along its mother's body and into a pouch

A red kangaroo joey peers from its mother's pouch as she feeds. Only male reds are actually red. Females are blue-gray and are sometimes called "blue fliers."

on her stomach. The baby drinks milk in the pouch and stays there until it has grown too big to fit inside. Mammals that raise their young like this are called **marsupials**.

Although they may look very different from one another, most kangaroos share the same basic way of life. They feed on leaves and grass, and since these are tough to chew and difficult to **digest**, kangaroos are specially **adapted**. They have big chewing teeth that are replaced as they wear down. And their stomachs contain **bacteria** that help break down the woody plant matter. This allows kangaroos to live in places where there is nothing to eat except grass.

Like all tree kangaroos, grizzled tree kangaroos are at home in the forest. Tree kangaroos are adapted to life in the trees and can leap up to 30 feet (9 m) from branch to branch.

Many kangaroos can also survive without drinking, which is very useful in the hot deserts of Australia. They get all the liquid they need from their food, and they avoid drying out too much by sheltering in the shade during the day. They usually come out to feed when the sun goes down and slip back into cover at daybreak. Because of this habit many of the smaller kangaroos can be hard to find, and some have stayed undiscovered until quite recently.

Despite their talent for survival in their natural **habitats**, many kangaroos are now endangered. When the Europeans came to Australia they brought sheep, goats, and rabbits with them. These destroyed the plants that many kangaroos feed on. The settlers cleared huge areas of **scrub** to create

A male gray kangaroo relaxes in the shade. Grays are the second-biggest kangaroos, after the red.

sheep pastures and fields for crops, so the smaller kangaroos had nowhere to shelter during the heat of the day. The forests were cut down, so tree kangaroos were left with nowhere to live. The Europeans also introduced foxes, dogs, and cats, which find small kangaroos easy to kill.

All this has been a disaster for many kangaroos. Most of the big kangaroos still do well, but some of the smaller ones are now very rare. At least five are already **extinct**, and several more now live only on small islands off the Australian coast. Luckily many people are now working hard to make sure kangaroos survive, so even the rarest ones may still have a future.

Kangaroos can be found in all sorts of places. Rocky slopes are home to these kangaroos, which are called unadorned rock wallabies.

Big Kangaroos

The most famous kangaroos are the red kangaroo and the two species of grays. One reason for this is their size, for they are by far the biggest. A male red kangaroo can weigh up to 190 pounds (86 kg) and grow to 8 feet (2.4 m) from nose to tail-tip, and a male gray can be almost as big.

Another reason why red and gray kangaroos are well known is that they live in large groups called **mobs**. Most kangaroos live alone and can be very secretive. But big mobs of gray and red kangaroos can often be seen feeding on open grassland in daylight.

A male red kangaroo hops across an open plain in Australia. The red is found in the drier parts of central and western Australia.

These big kangaroos have actually been helped by the changes people have made to the Australian landscape. Like sheep, they eat grass, so the huge sheep pastures created throughout Australia suit them very well. They like eating the kinds of grasses that sheep do not like, so they usually live alongside sheep without taking their food.

In very dry seasons, though, kangaroos and sheep compete for the same pasture, so most Australian sheep-farmers see kangaroos as pests. In the past, farmers shot as many as possible. This could be quite profitable, because they could sell the meat and skins. As a result, numbers of big kangaroos fell in some parts of their **ranges**. Today all kangaroos are protected by law, and licenses are needed if farmers want to shoot kangaroos as pests. Many big

Gray kangaroos feed on a golf course. These are eastern grays, which are found in Australia's eastern states. There is also the western gray, which lives in the south and southwest.

Area where the parma wallaby can be found

kangaroos are still killed every year. But it seems that the red and the grays are still quite plentiful and in no danger of becoming extinct at present.

Some of their close relatives have not been so lucky. The toolache wallaby, a particularly beautiful kangaroo that lived in swampy country in South Australia, was wiped out by 1927 because of hunting. Local farmers set their dogs on toolache wallabies to test their hunting skills, and unfortunately the dogs passed the test too well.

Another close relative of the red and gray kangaroos is the parma wallaby. Also known as the white-throated wallaby, it is dark brown on its back with a white throat and underparts and lives only in **rainforest** and scrub.

Though very closely related to the big kangaroos, the parma wallaby is much smaller. It is about 39 inches (1 m) from head to tail-tip and weighs up to 13 pounds (6 kg).

Much of this habitat was cleared by settlers in the nineteenth century, and numbers of parma wallabies began to fall. In 1932 this kangaroo was said to be extinct, but in 1965 a group of parma wallabies was discovered in New Zealand! A number had been taken there almost a century before, when they were still common in Australia. Scientists made plans to bring some back to their native land. Then, in 1967, more parma wallabies were found in the forests of eastern Australia, just north of Sydney. Parma wallabies are still rare in the wild, but happily there are plenty in zoos, so this kangaroo is safe for the moment.

Two male reds fight over a female at breeding time. They grab each other by the forelegs then use their back legs to try to push each other over.

Bridled nailtail wallaby
Black-footed rock wallaby
Brush-tailed rock wallaby
Proserpine rock wallaby
Yellow-footed rock wallaby

Areas where nailtail and rock wallabies can be found

Nailtail & Rock Wallabies

Nailtail wallabies get their name from the small, horny, nail-like tip on their tails. No one knows why they have this. When Europeans settled in Australia they found three species of nailtails. The crescent nailtail lived in central and western Australia, the bridled nailtail was plentiful in the open woodlands of the east, and the northern nailtail lived on the wooded grasslands of the north.

Once thought to be extinct, the bridled nailtail was discovered again in 1973.

Although it is the same shape as a big kangaroo, a nailtail wallaby is much smaller. Males can grow to about 4 feet (1.2 m) long from head to tail-tip and weigh up to 12 pounds (5.5 kg). Like most smaller kangaroos, nailtails usually live alone. They hide in the bushes by day in shallow holes that they dig with their long front claws. As night falls, they come out to feed on grass.

The northern nailtail is still common throughout much of northern Australia, but the other two species have suffered very badly from changes made to their habitats. Because they rely on thick undergrowth for cover during the day,

An unadorned rock wallaby shelters in a cave with its long tail between its legs. Rock wallabies' feet have rough soles to give them a good grip on the slippery rock.

15

they have disappeared from huge areas that have been cleared of trees and scrub. The bridled nailtail now lives only in a small region of central Queensland, where it survives in a protected area. But the crescent nailtail has not been seen since the 1950s and is now probably extinct.

The rock wallabies have been luckier, mainly because they live in places that do not make good farmland. About the same size as the nailtails, they live in rocky country where caves and cracks provide shelter from the sun. At dusk they come out, leaping across the rocks with amazing agility to reach areas of lush grass, where they feed.

Scientists are not sure how many species of rock wallabies exist, but there are thought to be about ten. Rock

A yellow-footed rock wallaby sits on a rock, just like a little person. This kangaroo has beautiful markings and is sometimes called the ring-tailed rock wallaby.

Some rock wallabies have patterned coats to help them blend in among the rocks. This is a black-footed rock wallaby, with a joey peeking out of her pouch.

wallabies are hunted by large **birds of prey**, such as the wedge-tailed eagle. But this has been happening for thousands of years, and the rock wallabies have managed to survive. Far worse for these kangaroos are the goats that were brought to Australia about 200 years ago and now run wild. Goats are well equipped for life on rocky hills and compete with the rock wallabies for food and shelter.

As a result, several species of rock wallabies are now becoming rare. Among these is the yellow-footed rock wallaby of eastern Australia, which has also been hunted for its skin and is eaten by foxes. Other threatened species include the brush-tailed and the black-footed rock wallabies. The most endangered rock wallaby of all is the proserpine rock wallaby of Queensland. Believe it or not, this kangaroo was not discovered until 1976!

Banded hare wallaby
Spectacled hare wallaby
Western hare wallaby

AUSTRALIA

Tasmania

Areas where hare wallabies can be found

Hare Wallabies

When Europeans started to explore Australia in the late eighteenth century, some of the creatures they found reminded them of animals they knew back home. Among them was a small wallaby that looked and behaved rather like a hare. It was about the same size, just as fast, and amazingly agile. It lived alone in open country and usually spent the day in the shade of a grass tussock, just like a hare. They called it a hare wallaby.

Though it looks similar to the larger kangaroos, the western hare wallaby is tiny – only 15 inches (38 cm) tall.

Eventually it became known as the eastern hare wallaby, because three more species were discovered. These were the western, spectacled, and banded hare wallabies. One explorer found another in the middle of the Australian **outback**, but the central hare wallaby, as it was called, has never been seen again. Although it may be living out there somewhere, it has probably become extinct, because that is what has happened to most of the others.

Before the Europeans arrived, the Australian **aborigines** used to set fire to small patches of grassland to destroy old tussocks and make new shoots grow. A number of creatures, including hare wallabies, like to eat these young,

The spectacled hare wallaby gets its name from the orange ring around its eye. It makes the animal look as though it is wearing eyeglasses.

juicy shoots, and the aborigines knew this. When the animals came out at night to eat the new grass, the people would catch them for food. They never caught many, though, only enough for their needs, so the kangaroos were never in danger of dying out.

After European farmers drove the aborigines from their land, however, the grass and scrub kept growing until it was destroyed by bushfires. These burnt much more fiercely than the small fires started by the aborigines. Instead of causing new shoots to grow, the bushfires destroyed many plants completely. They also killed many of the animals. The foxes and cats brought by the settlers hunted and ate the survivors, and the little hare wallabies started disappearing.

This western hare wallaby is sheltering beneath a tussock of spinifex grass – its main food in the Tanami Desert of central Australia.

By 1890, the eastern hare wallaby was extinct, and by 1906 the banded hare wallaby had vanished from mainland Australia. Numbers of western hare wallabies, however, did not start to fall until the 1940s. Today the survivors live in a very small area of the Tanami Desert, in central Australia, and on two islands in the far west where they are safe from foxes and cats. These islands are also the home of the only surviving banded hare wallabies. The spectacled hare wallaby is the only species that is still widespread.

The spectacled hare wallaby gets all the liquid it needs from its food. It does not drink, even when there is water around.

The surviving hare wallabies are now carefully protected. In parts of central Australia the land is now burned using the old aborigine method. Scientists hope that this will help the western hare wallaby stage a comeback.

Goodfellow's tree kangaroo
Grizzled tree kangaroo
Lumholtz's tree kangaroo

New Guinea
AUSTRALIA
Tasmania

Areas where tree kangaroos can be found

Tree Kangaroos

If you visited New Guinea, just north of Australia, and explored the thick rainforest that covers most of the island, you would come across some wonderful creatures. Birds of paradise display their dazzling colors in the branches. Spiny, porcupine-like animals called echidnas (e-KID-nas) snuffle through the dead leaves on the ground looking for worms. Enormous birdwing butterflies glide through the forest glades. But most surprising of all are the kangaroos that live in trees.

A Lumholtz's tree kangaroo sits in a rainforest tree in Queensland, Australia. This is a young male about 8 months old.

Why would a kangaroo climb a tree? The reason is that in the forests of New Guinea there is more food in the trees than on the ground. So over millions of years some of the local kangaroos became adapted to reach it. The back legs and feet of tree kangaroos are much shorter than those of typical kangaroos, and their front legs are longer and stronger. This means they can use all four limbs to cling to the branches. They are the only kangaroos able to move their back legs alternately. All others have to move both back legs at one time except when they are swimming.

Despite these adaptations tree kangaroos move clumsily in the trees. Yet they have survived because they have few natural enemies and they are the only big leaf-eating

Goodfellow's tree kangaroos clamber around in the forests of New Guinea. Tree kangaroos' feet have rough, cushioned soles to grip the bark.

Areas where tree
kangaroos can
be found

animals in the New Guinea forests. They have even spread to Australia. Long ago, tree kangaroos found their way to the rainforests of the Australian state of Queensland. They still live there today.

There are two species of tree kangaroos in Queensland, and at least seven in New Guinea. There may be more, because two were discovered only very recently in the dense rainforest. Many are named after the people who discovered them, including Goodfellow's and Doria's tree kangaroos. One of the bigger ones, Bennett's tree kangaroo, can weigh up to 28 pounds (13 kg) and grow up to about 5 feet (1.5 m) long from head to tail-tip.

A Doria's tree kangaroo stands on the forest floor. Although tree kangaroos can walk along branches, when they are on the ground they hop, just like other kangaroos.

Unfortunately all tree kangaroos are threatened by the cutting down of their forest homes. The Australian species live in a small area of surviving rainforest on the northeast coast. Although the kangaroos are protected in special **reserves**, the forest is still being felled for timber. On New Guinea there are a lot more trees, but they are being cut down much faster. So it may not be long before some of the New Guinea species have nowhere to live. Many people are trying to stop this happening, though, and preserve these dark, mysterious forests and all the wonderful creatures that live in them.

Matschie's tree kangaroo lives in the forests of eastern New Guinea. Like most kangaroos, tree kangaroos feed by night. They usually spend the day asleep in the trees.

Areas where rat kangaroos can be found

Rat Kangaroos

The smallest kangaroos are hardly bigger than rats, so not surprisingly the early settlers called them rat kangaroos. There are about ten species, and most of them behave much like their larger relatives. They hop around on their long back legs like other kangaroos, shelter in dense undergrowth by day, and feed mainly at night.

Many rat kangaroos have unusual names – there are potoroos, bettongs, the woylie, and the boodie. Most live in fairly open country, where all the problems that affect other

A kind of rat kangaroo, the rufous bettong lives in the open forests of eastern Australia, where it is, happily, still common.

kangaroos have come together to make life almost impossible for them. Farmers have cleared away much of the undergrowth that they sheltered in, and rabbits, goats, and bushfires have destroyed a lot more. Only two species are still common over large areas, and two have vanished altogether. The others have disappeared from most of the places where they used to live.

One of the rat kangaroos that has become rare is the woylie. About 30 inches (76 cm) long, including its tail, this tiny kangaroo spends the day hidden in a little grass nest. When night falls, the woylie comes out to feed, wrapping its tail around its home and carrying it about as it eats. The woylie is able to survive the bushfires that destroy its habitat from time to time, but it is no match for the fox.

The woylie used to be found over much of southern Australia. It now survives only on the southwest tip and on one or two small islands.

Rat Kangaroos

Two of the rat kangaroos survive only on islands. The Tasmanian bettong once lived in southeast Australia, but today is found only on Tasmania where there is plenty of open forest, few rabbits, and hardly any foxes. About 12 inches (30 cm) long, with a tail of the same length, it can weigh up to 5 pounds (2.2 kg).

The other island species is the boodie. Slightly larger than the Tasmanian bettong, it is the only kangaroo that always sleeps in a burrow. It lives in groups, in a system of tunnels like a rabbit warren. By staying underground all day, the boodie avoids the sun. This once allowed it to live in the hottest parts of western Australia. Its burrows could not protect it from foxes, though, and today it survives only on a few fox-free islands off Australia's west coast.

A baby long-nosed potoroo and its mother feed in the undergrowth. Like many rat kangaroos, the long-nosed potoroo has become extinct in some areas in which it used to live.

Now that more Australians are becoming concerned about wildlife, the future for this red kangaroo joey is looking a lot brighter.

Although the big kangaroos are still plentiful, many of the smaller ones are vanishing fast as their habitats are destroyed by farming and forestry. Until recently, most Australians had no idea that so many of their wild animals were endangered. But the more people learn about wildlife, the more they are concerned about what is happening. They are setting up new wildlife reserves and stopping projects that threaten the future of kangaroos and other wild animals. So although some kangaroos are now extremely rare, there is hope for their future.

Useful Addresses

For more information about kangaroos and how you can help protect them, contact these organizations:

Conservation International
1015 18th Street NW
Washington, D.C. 20037

Defenders of Wildlife
1244 19th Street NW
Washington, D.C. 20036

Metro Toronto Zoo
361A Old Finch Ave
Scarborough, ON
M1B 5K7

U.S. Fish and Wildlife Service
Endangered Species and Habitat
Conservation
400 Arlington Square
18th and C Streets NW
Washington, D.C. 20240

**Wildlife Preservation Trust
International**
3400 W. Girard Avenue
Philadelphia, PA 19104

World Wildlife Fund
1250 24th Street NW
Washington, D.C. 20037

Further Reading

Endangered Animals George S. Fichter (New York: Golden Press, 1995)

Endangered Species Lynn M. Stone (Chicago: Childrens Press, 1984)

Endangered Wildlife of the World (New York: Marshall Cavendish Corporation, 1993)

Kangaroos Denise Burt (Boston: Houghton-Mifflin, 1991)

Kangaroos Emilie U. Lepthien (Chicago: Childrens Press, 1995)

Kangaroos and Other Marsupials Norman Barrett (New York: Franklin Watts, 1991)

Kangaroos on Location Kathy Darling (New York: Lothrop, Lee & Shepard, 1993)

Wildlife of the World (New York: Marshall Cavendish Corporation, 1994)

Glossary

Aborigines (Ab-o-RIDGE-in-ees): The Australian people, who arrived in Australia at least 50,000 years before Europeans.

Adapt: To change in order to survive in new conditions.

Bacteria (Back-TEAR-ee-a): Tiny lifeforms found in the stomachs of animals, as well as in many other places.

Bird of prey: A type of bird that usually has a hooked bill and clawed feet and hunts and eats other animals.

Digest: To turn food in the stomach into substances that an animal's body needs to survive.

Evolve: To develop over a long period of time.

Extinct (Ex-TINKT): No longer living anywhere in the world.

Habitat: The place where an animal lives. For example, Lumholtz's tree kangaroo's habitat is the rainforest.

Mammal: A kind of animal that is warm-blooded and has a backbone. Most are covered with fur or have hair. Females have glands that produce milk to feed their young.

Marsupial (Mar-SOU-pee-al): A kind of mammal whose young are born tiny and then develop inside pouches on their mothers' stomachs.

Mob: The name given to a large group of big kangaroos.

Outback: The wilderness areas of Australia, away from the cities.

Rainforest: A forest that has heavy rainfall much of the year.

Range: The area in the world in which a particular species of animal can be found.

Reserve: Land that has been set aside where plants and animals can live without being harmed.

Scrub: Land that is covered by low trees and shrubs.

Species: A kind of animal or plant. For example, the red kangaroo is a species of kangaroo.

Index